WADE ZAHARES

BIG, BAD
and a little bit
SCARY

poems that bite back!

SCHOLASTIC INC.
New York Toronto London Auckland Sydney
Mexico City New Delhi Hong Kong Buenos Aires

Always Be Kind to Animals

Always be kind to animals
Morning, noon and night.
For animals have feelings too,
And furthermore they bite!

John Gardner

Viper

Viper, viper
spiteful sniper,
snake in the grass, lowdown, base,
smiling, smiling to your face,
virulent villain, venomous, vile,
darting poison with a snaky smile.

Eve Merriam

Alligator

Old bull of the waters,
old dinosaur cousin,
with scales by the hundreds
and teeth by the dozen,

old singer of swamp lands,
old slithery swimmer,
what do you dream of
when fireflies glimmer?

Can you remember
the folk tales of old
when you breathed fire
and guarded the gold

and stole lovely ladies
and captured their kings
and flew over mountains
on magical wings?

Old bull of the waters,
how can you know
men made you a dragon
in dreams, long ago?

Maxine W. Kumin

The Panther

The panther is like a leopard,
Except it hasn't been peppered.
Should you behold a panther crouch,
Prepare to say Ouch.
Better yet, if called by a panther,
Don't anther.

Ogden Nash

The Sparrow Hawk

Wings like pistols flashing at his sides,
Masked, above the meadow runway rides,
Galloping, galloping with an easy rein.
Below, the field mouse, where the shadow glides,
Holds fast the small purse of his life, and hides.

Russell Hoban

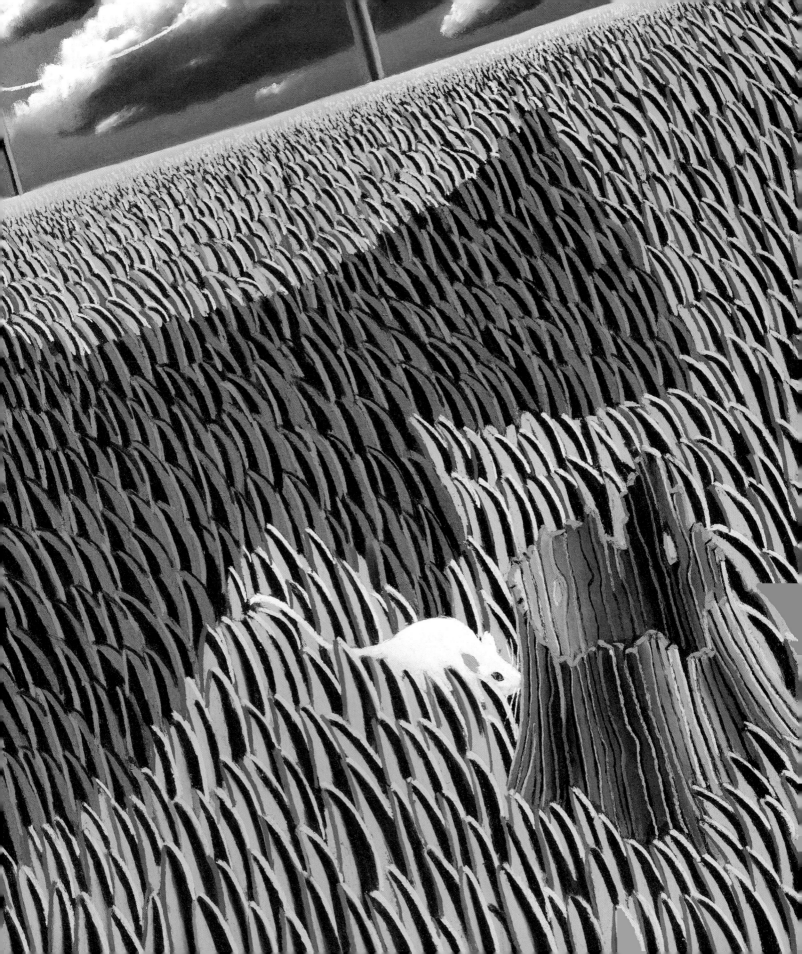

A treacherous monster is the Shark,
He never makes the least remark.
And when he sees you on the sand,
He doesn't seem to want to land.
He watches you take off your clothes,
And not the least excitement shows.
His eyes do not grow bright or roll,
He has astounding self-control.
He waits till you are quite undressed,
And seems to take no interest.
And when towards the sea you leap,
He looks as if he were asleep.
But when you once get in his range,
His whole demeanor seems to change.
He throws his body right about,
And his true character comes out.
It's no use crying or appealing,
He seems to lose all decent feeling.
After this warning you will wish
To keep clear of this treacherous fish.
His back is black, his stomach white,
He has a very dangerous bite.

Lord Alfred Douglas

Lion

Look!
A lion!
Mighty beast.
    (Might he
    Bite me
    For a feast?)

Though
I know
He wouldn't dare,
    I'm mighty glad

he's over there.

Mary Ann Hoberman

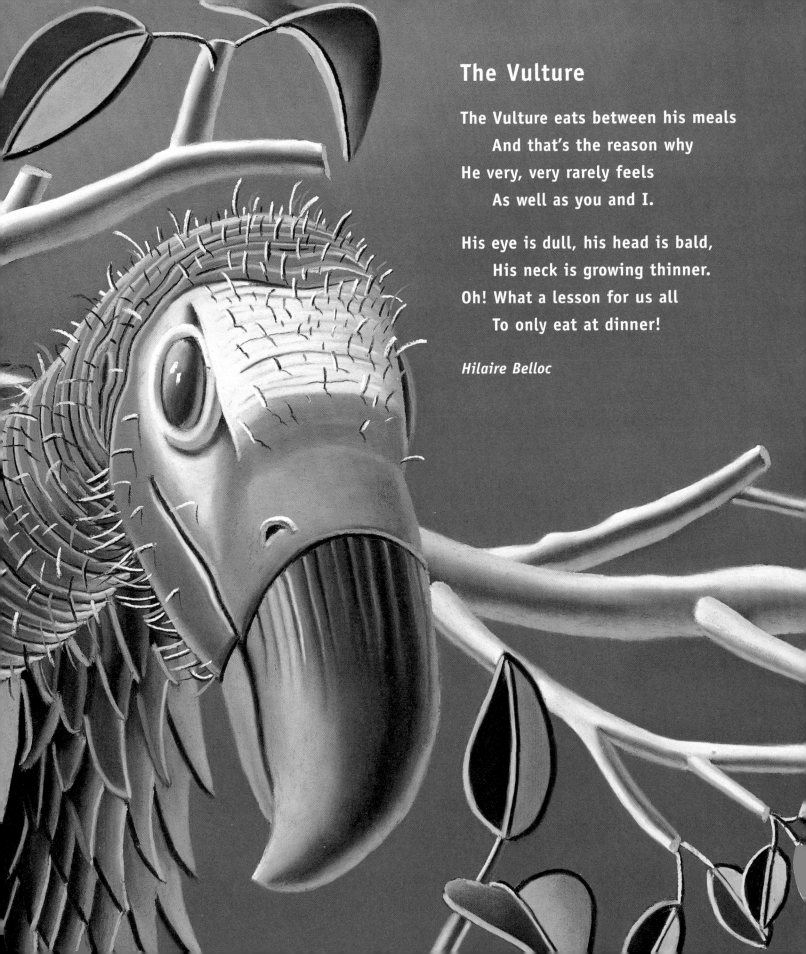

The Vulture

The Vulture eats between his meals
    And that's the reason why
He very, very rarely feels
    As well as you and I.

His eye is dull, his head is bald,
    His neck is growing thinner.
Oh! What a lesson for us all
    To only eat at dinner!

Hilaire Belloc

The Eel

The feel
Of an eel
Is slippery,
Slimy;
He's sleek
And he's black
As a panther
At night.
He slides
Through your fingers
Rapidly,
Slyly;
A flip
Of his tail
And he slips
Out of sight.

Robert S. Oliver

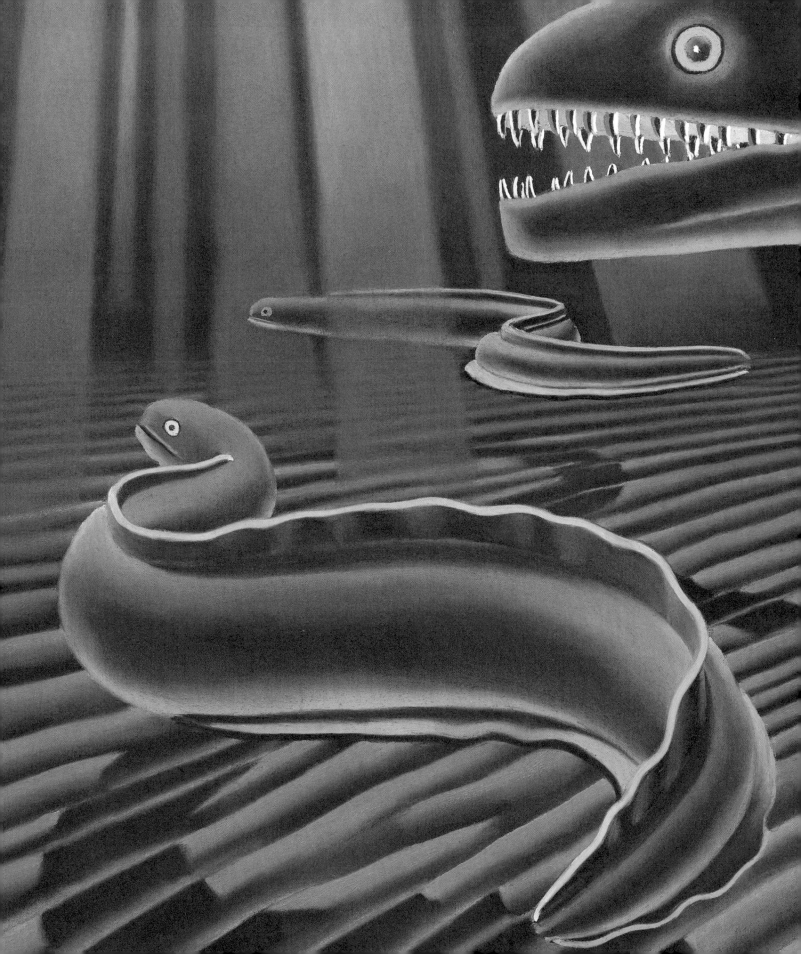

The Porcupine

A porcupine looks somewhat silly.
He also is extremely quilly.
And if he shoots a quill at you,
Run fast
Or you'll be quilly too.

I would not want a porcupine
To be my loving valentine.

Karla Kuskin

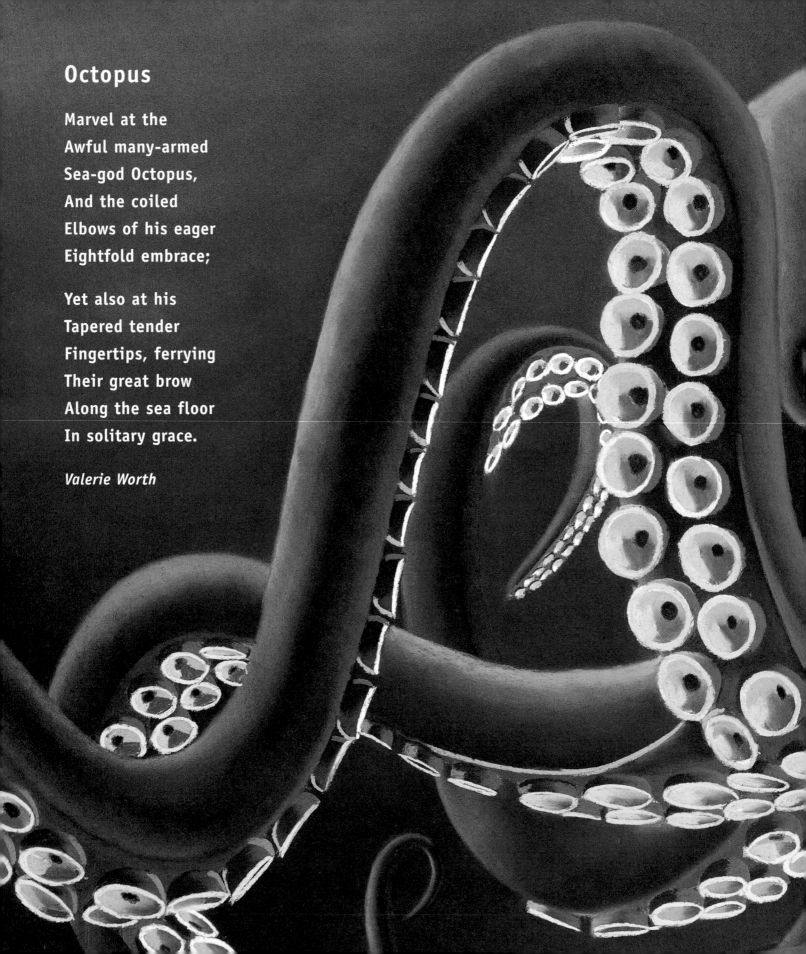

Octopus

Marvel at the
Awful many-armed
Sea-god Octopus,
And the coiled
Elbows of his eager
Eightfold embrace;

Yet also at his
Tapered tender
Fingertips, ferrying
Their great brow
Along the sea floor
In solitary grace.

Valerie Worth

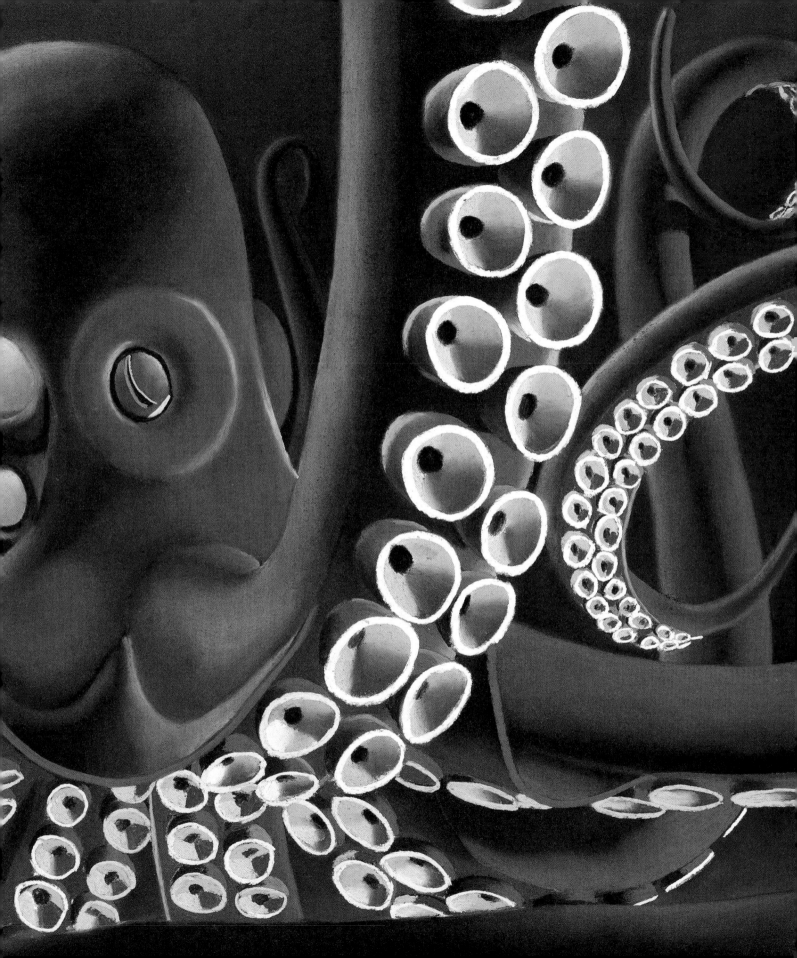

Strippers

If you fall into a river that's full of Piranha,
They'll strip off your flesh like you'd skin a banana.
There's no time for screaming, there's no time for groans.

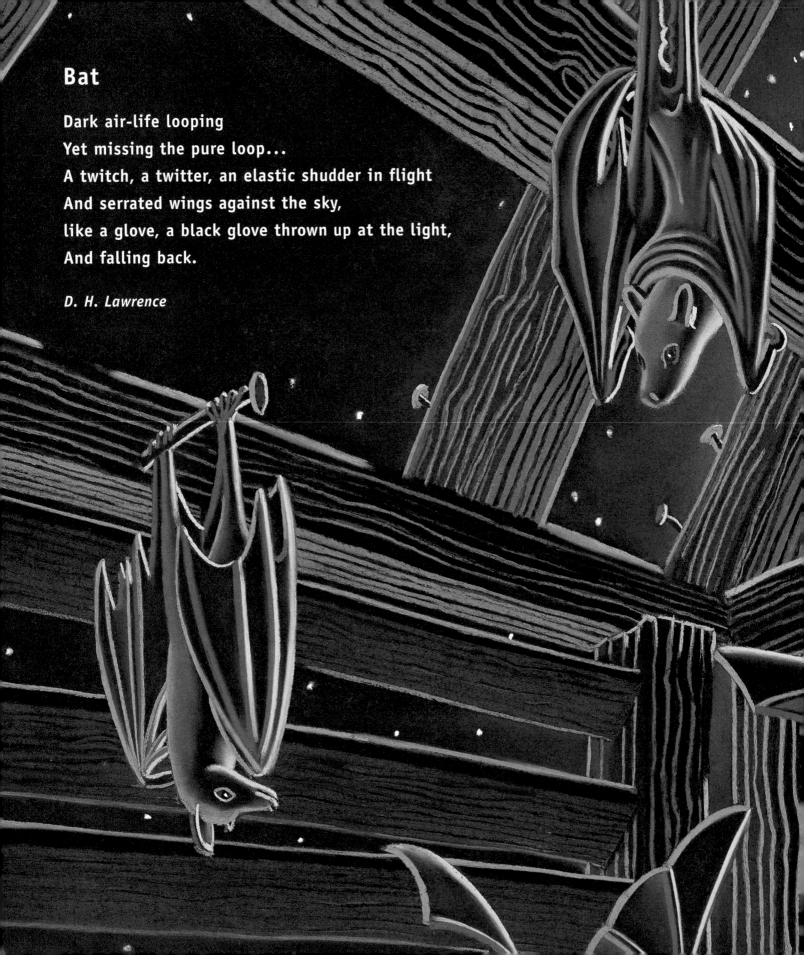

Bat

Dark air-life looping
Yet missing the pure loop...
A twitch, a twitter, an elastic shudder in flight
And serrated wings against the sky,
like a glove, a black glove thrown up at the light,
And falling back.

D. H. Lawrence

The Barracuda

Slowly, slowly he cruises,
And slowly, slowly he chooses
Which kind of fish he prefers to take this morning;
Then without warning
The Barracuda opens his jaws, teeth flashing,
And with a horrible, horrible grinding and gnashing,
Devours a hundred poor creatures and feels no remorse.
It's no wonder of course,
That he really ought, perhaps, to change his ways.
"But" (as he says
With an evil grin)
"It's actually not my fault, you see!
I've nothing to do with the tragedy;
I open my mouth for a yawn and—ah me—
They all
    swim
        in."

John Gardner

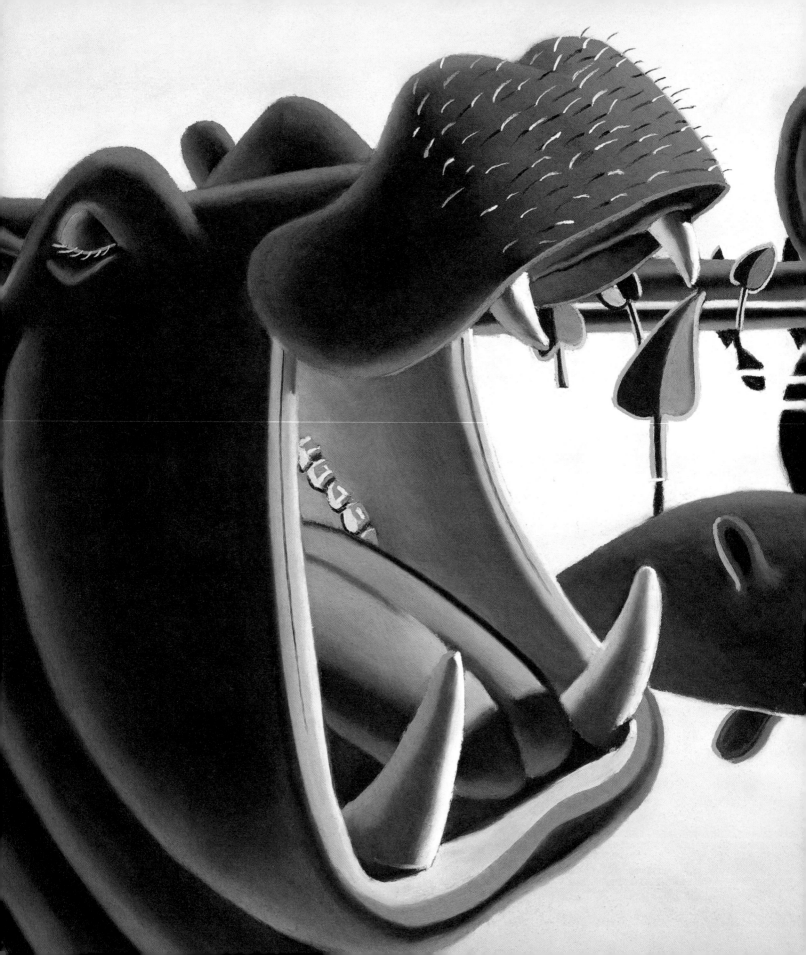

Hippopotamus

The Hippopotamus—Hippo for short—
Is as lazy as sin, it is sad to report.
He wallows for hours up to his eyes
In mud while tropical Butterflies
Flicker above him through the skies,
While Peacocks scream and Apes cavort.
Black water trickles down from his ears,
Around his head the blue mist clears;
He lifts his broad back, shakes off flies,
Opens his pink mouth, blinks his eyes,
Then sinks back under, and disappears.

William Jay Smith

This book is for you, Judy Sue
—W.Z.

Grateful acknowledgment is given to the following for permission to reprint previously published material:

"Always Be Kind to Animals" from *A Child's Bestiary*, by John Gardner. Copyright © 1977 Boskydell Artists, Ltd. Reprinted by permission of Georges Borchardt, Inc., for the author. • "Viper" reprinted with the permission of Simon & Schuster Books for Young Readers, an imprint of Simon & Schuster Children's Publishing Division from *Halloween ABC* by Eve Merriam. Text copyright © 1987 Eve Merriam. • "Alligator" by Maxine Kumin. Copyright © 1962 by Maxine Kumin. Reprinted by permission of the author. • "The Panther" by Ogden Nash. Copyright © 1940 by Ogden Nash. Reprinted by permission of Curtis Brown, Ltd. • "The Sparrow Hawk" by Russell Hoban from *The Pedaling Man*. Copyright © 1968. Reprinted by permission of David Higham Associates. • "The Shark" by Lord Alfred Douglas. • "The Lion" by Mary Ann Hoberman. Reprinted by permission of Gina Maccoby Literary Agency copyright © 1973 by Mary Ann Hoberman. • "The Vulture" by Hilaire Belloc. Reprinted by permission of PFD on behalf of the Estate of Hilaire Belloc. Copyright © Hilaire Belloc, 1910, 1973. • "The Eel" reprinted with the permission of Atheneum Books for Young Readers, an imprint of Simon & Schuster Children's Publishing Division from *Cornucopia*, by Robert S. Oliver. Copyright © 1978 Robert S. Oliver • "The Porcupine" by Karla Kuskin. Copyright © 1962, 1980 by Karla Kuskin. Reprinted by permission of Scott Treimel, NY. • "octopus" reprinted by permission of Farrar, Straus and Giroux, LLC from *Small Poems Again* by Valerie Worth. Copyright © 1986 by Valerie Worth. • "Strippers" by Dick King-Smith. Text copyright © Fox Busters Ltd., 1990. Extracted from *Jungle Jingles* by Dick King-Smith, published by Doubleday, a division of Transworld Publishers. All rights reserved. • "Bat" by D. H. Lawrence, from *The Complete Poems of D. H. Lawrence* by D. H. Lawrence, edited by V. de Sola Pinto & F. W. Roberts, copyright © 1964, 1971 by Angelo Ravagli and C. M. Weekley, Executors of the Estate of Frieda Lawrence Ravagli. Used by permission of Viking Penguin, a division of Penguin Putnam Inc. • "The Barracuda" from *A Child's Bestiary*, by John Gardner. Copyright © 1977 Boskydell Artists, Ltd. Reprinted by permission of Georges Borchardt, Inc., for the author. • "Hippopotamus" reprinted by permission of Farrar, Straus and Giroux, LLC from *Laughing Time: Collected Nonsense* by William Jay Smith. Copyright © 1990 by William Jay Smith.

ISBN 0-439-44216-8

12 11 10 9 8 7 6 5 4 3 2   3 4 5 6 7/0

Printed in the U.S.A.   09

First Scholastic printing, November 2002

The art is rendered in pastel on paper.

Set in ITC Officina Sans
Book design by Angela Carlino